Publis

This second special volume
found by a rambler at the b
recognised Charlie's writing
posted the journal straight to the publisher...
astounding adventure.

There must be other notebooks to find, so please keep your eyes peeled. If you do come across an amazing diary, or see an eight-year-old boy riding a hovering scooter, please let us know.

NAME: Charlie Small

ADDRESS: Chasm of the Killer Bees

AGE: 400!

MOBILE: 07713 12

SCHOOL: St Beckham's

THINGS I LIKE: My Spider-thread Wristband; Bron; honey

THINGS I HATE: Badland crabs; monster bees; bottomless chasms.

OUR LADY OF DOLOURS SCHOOL
19 CIRENCESTER STREET
LONDON W2 5SR

THE AMAZING ADVENTURES OF CHARLIE SMALL (400)

Special Notebook 2

Chasm of The Killer Bees

Published by Pearson Education Limited, Edinburgh Gate, Harlow, Essex, CM20 2JE
Registered company number: 872828

www.pearsonschools.co.uk

Text © Charlie Small 2011

Designed by Bigtop
Original illustrations © Charlie Small
Illustrated by Charlie Small

The right of Charlie Small to be identified as author of this work has been asserted by him in accordance with the Copyright, Designs and Patents Act 1988.

First published 2011 by Pearson Education Limited

Based on The Amazing Adventures of Charlie Small series published in Great Britain by David Fickling Books, a division of Random House Children's Books, A Random House Company.

15 14 13 12
10 9 8 7 6 5 4 3

British Library Cataloguing in Publication Data
A catalogue record for this book is available from the British Library

ISBN 978 1 408 27403 3

Copyright notice
All rights reserved. No part of this publication may be reproduced in any form or by any means (including photocopying or storing it in any medium by electronic means and whether or not transiently or incidentally to some other use of this publication) without the written permission of the copyright owner, except in accordance with the provisions of the Copyright, Designs and Patents Act 1988 or under the terms of a licence issued by the Copyright Licensing Agency, Saffron House, 6–10 Kirby Street, London EC1N 8TS (www.cla.co.uk). Applications for the copyright owner's written permission should be addressed to the publisher.

Printed and bound in Malaysia, CTP-PJB

Acknowledgements
We would like to thank the children and teachers of Bangor Central Integrated Primary School, NI; Bishop Henderson C of E Primary School, Somerset; Brookside Community Primary School, Somerset; Cheddington Combined School, Buckinghamshire; Cofton Primary School, Birmingham; Dair House Independent School, Buckinghamshire; Deal Parochial School, Kent; Newbold Riverside Primary School, Rugby and Windmill Primary School, Oxford for their invaluable help in the development and trialling of the Bug Club resources.

Every effort has been made to contact copyright holders of material reproduced in this book. Any omissions will be rectified in subsequent printings if notice is given to the publishers.

If you find this book, PLEASE look after it. This is the only true account of my remarkable adventures.

My name is Charlie Small and I am four hundred years old, but in all those long years, I have never grown up. Something happened when I was eight years old. Something I can't begin to understand. I went on a journey... and I'm still trying to find my way home. Now, although I've had four hundred years of perilous adventures, I still look like any eight-year-old boy you might pass in the street.

During my amazing adventures I've robbed a mummy's tomb, defeated a giant Rat King in open warfare and lots, lots more. You may think this sounds fantastic. You could think it's a lie, but you would be wrong. Because EVERYTHING IN THIS BOOK IS TRUE. Believe this single fact and you can share the most incredible journey ever experienced.   Charlie Small

Crossing Swords With Creepy Crustaceans

I don't believe it! I'm in trouble again and having to write up my journal in the most perilous position ever! I'm well and truly trapped, halfway down a … no, let me explain *everything* in the right order.

I'd been scooting for hours across a bleak landscape on my hover-scooter, the Air-rider. (It had been a gift from my pal Jakeman, an incredible inventor whose marvellous machines have helped me loads of times on my adventures.) Huge cracks, metres wide, crisscrossed the ground making it look like an enormous jigsaw puzzle. I steered a weaving path between the gaps.

It was late afternoon and I needed to find somewhere to sleep for the night. I brought the Air-rider to a halt and scanned the landscape through my telescope. I couldn't see anywhere to shelter so, hunching my shoulders against the stinging wind, I prepared to set off again. It was then that I heard a loud scrabbling noise coming from one of the great cracks in the ground.

To my horror a huge, saw-edged claw emerged, crumbling away the hard mud at the edges of the crack. Seconds later, a monstrous, blue-backed crab crawled out of the ground and turned to face me. *Oh jeepers!* It was as big as a car! Then, with more scraping and scuffing from underfoot, masses of the razor-clawed monsters climbed out of the ground and stood on spiky tiptoes all around me.

They had beady, bloodshot eyes that waved about on stalks. Their massive, curved claws looked powerful enough to snap a tree trunk, and their domed backs shone like polished metal. With a clattering of spiky legs they rushed towards me, scuttling sideways like monstrous armoured frisbees. In a cold sweat, I fired up the scooter and tried to steer through them, my heart hammering against my chest.

I twisted and turned, ducking to avoid their snapping claws. *Yikes!* One of those things could snip my leg right off. I drew the broken sword I had slung around my waist and struck the crabs' powerful pincers.

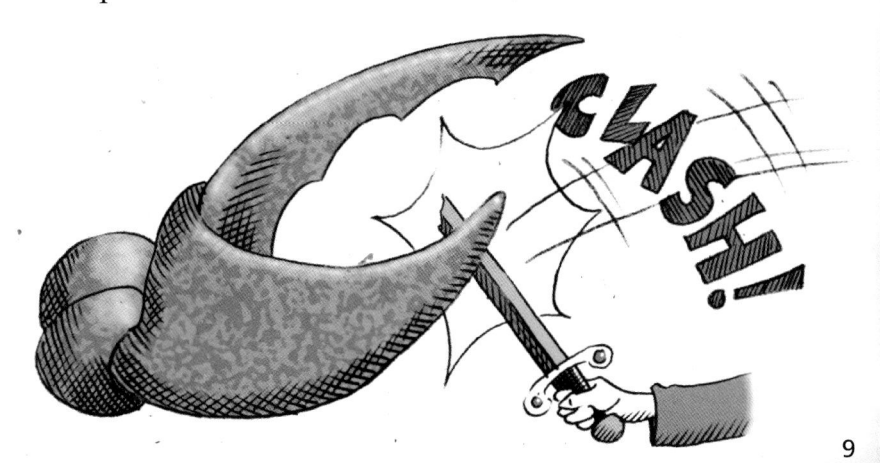

Crack! Whack! I brought the sword crashing down, again and again, on their domed backs. The blade just slid and sparked across their shells, but the crabs dropped back and for a split second a path opened up before me. I twisted the scooter's throttle and, shaking like a jelly, whizzed away. The crabs quickly recovered, but my scooter could do 65 kilometres an hour. I managed to outpace them and eventually left the clacking crustaceans far behind. I was still congratulating myself on a narrow escape, when I suddenly had to screech to a halt!

I shook like a jelly!

Falling To My Doom

A great, jagged chasm snaked across the ground as far as the eye could see. It was as wide as a football pitch and so deep that I couldn't see the bottom. The sheer

A great chasm snaked across the ground.

walls of rock fell away into murky shadows and thin, ragged clouds floated below me.

Now I could hear the faint clackety-clack of the crabs again. They hadn't given up their chase and it looked like they had me cornered. I raced along the edge of the chasm, trying to find a way across. Then, in the distance, I saw a great arch of stone rising up from my side of the chasm. *It's a bridge!* I thought. But as I got closer I saw that the arch had broken away in the middle.

"What can I do?" I cried in a panic, for now I could see the crabs – and they could see me. There was only one thing for it. I revved up my scooter and did a wide circle to gather speed. With the crabs now snapping at my heels, I raced straight for the broken arch.

Up and up I zoomed and then *whoosh!* I rocketed from the end and flew across the gap like a daredevil stunt rider. Down and down I soared towards the far arm of the arch. Would I make it – would I?

"Yee-hah!" I bellowed, as my Air-rider just landed on the opposite section of the bridge. Then, *"Whoa!"* I screamed, as it crumbled beneath me and I tumbled over and over, deep down into the chasm below.

The Tree Of Life

The air grew chilly as I fell. *I'm done for,* I thought. *This is where my adventures end.* Then, *WHACK!* I hit something hard and was knocked senseless.

When I came to, I found myself caught in the leafy branches of a great tree that grew horizontally from the side of the chasm.

What are the chances of that happening? I wondered, and rubbed my sore head.

I stood up carefully on the wide trunk of the tree and looked around. The dark wall of the chasm soared above me and was pitted with hundreds of small caves. Sat in a cave above the base of the tree was a young but ferocious-looking bear. If he stood upright, he would only come up to my chest, but he was strong and had a large jaw of sharp teeth. Long claws curved from paws as big as baseball mitts!

Grabbed!

"Grrll, grrnrr grr … fell!" the bear snarled, leaping from the cave mouth and padding menacingly towards me along the tree trunk. I took a couple of steps backwards.

"Nice bear," I said, trying to sound confident.

The young bear padded towards me.

"Grr … fell," the bear growled again, drawing back his lips to reveal terrible yellow fangs. I took another step back. The bear kept coming towards me until he was close enough to touch. Then, as I edged back again, my foot slipped. I grabbed at a branch but it snapped off in my hand and I fell from the tree.

"Help!" I yelled, but instantly a large paw grabbed my wrist in a powerful grip. The next second I had been hauled effortlessly back onto the tree and found myself nose to nose with the bear. He was sniffing at me curiously.

"Thanks!" I gasped, as the bear continued to sniff and snuffle.

"Grr … fell," he said, looking up towards the bridge high above our heads. I realised the bear was trying to speak like a human. It was just that his voice growled so much that he was hard to understand!

"You fell too?" I said.

A large paw grabbed my wrist.

"Grrr!" he growled, nodding his large head. "Brrridge brrroke. Pa … grrr … safe. I … grrr … fell," he said.

"Your Pa's up there?" I asked, as I followed his sad gaze upwards. "Can't he help us?"

"No … grrr … way … down … grrr. No … grrr … way … up … grrr," growled the bear. Looking about, I could believe him. Below our feet there was a sheer drop to nothing. Way above us, the top of the chasm looked like a thin, jagged line of soft light. We were well and truly stranded. Evening was already upon us and it looked as if I was going to have to spend the night in the chasm.

"Bron!" said the bear, slapping his hairy chest with a great paw. "Bron!"

"And I'm Charlie Small," I said. "Pleased to meet you, Bron."

We talked late into the evening and Bron clumsily prepared a supper of crispy plant roots dipped in golden, runny honey. They were delicious, but where on earth did he find honey in this gloomy place?

Crispy root dipped in honey yum!

Time For Bed

That's how I found myself writing up my journal, stuck halfway down a chasm. I'm stretched out on a fern-covered floor in Bron's cave, ready for sleep and with a tummy fit to burst. Bron is already snoring his head off. He sounds like an old motorbike, but his thick, soft fur is keeping me lovely and warm. He is a gentle creature but I wouldn't want to get on the wrong side of those claws!

I wonder how we are *ever* going to get out of this chasm? Goodnight!

Phoning Home

It's no good. I just can't sleep. My mind is spinning with ideas that go nowhere, and I need to hear the sound of a friendly voice. I think I'll call Mum on my wind-up mobile.

"Oh, hello, darling, is everything all right?" asked Mum, when she answered.

"Yes, Mum, everything's fine, except I'm stuck in a bottomless chasm with no way out and only a ferocious wild bear for company," I said.

"Sounds wonderful, dear," said Mum, cheerily. "Oh, wait a minute, Charlie. Here's your dad just come in. Now remember, don't be late for tea, and if you're passing the shops on the way back, please pick up a carton of milk. Bye."

"Yes, Mum," I said as she hung up.

It's always good to hear her voice, even if she does say the same thing *every* time I call. I've been gone for four hundred years and she's *still* expecting me home in time for tea!

I'm wide awake now. I wonder if my wild animal collector's cards have anything to say about the giant crabs that attacked me. *Yikes!* Yes, they do.

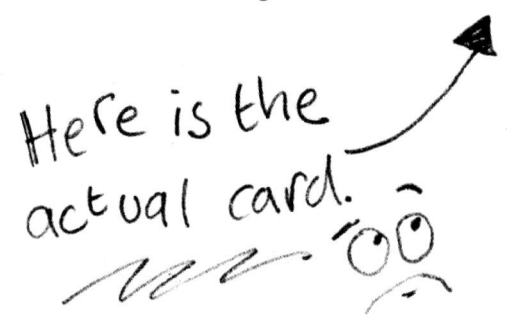

Here is the actual card.

PREDATOR RATING 12

Badland Crabs

Armour-plated crustaceans that have evolved into monsters over millions of years. They are fast, aggressive hunters and their claws can crush a car. They live on buffalo, bear and humans.

Escape on foot is impossible.

WILD ANIMAL COLLECTOR'S CARDS

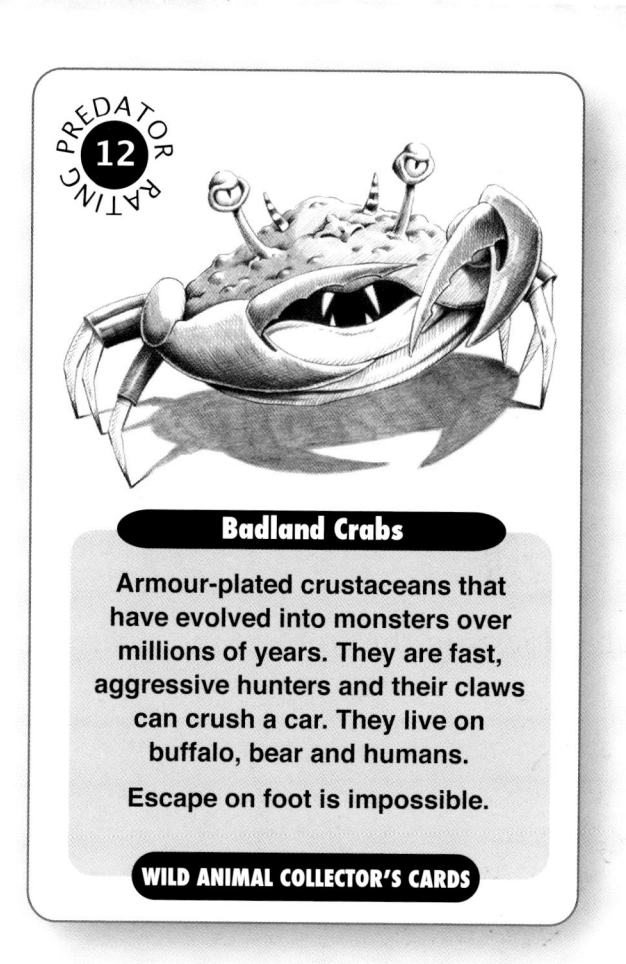

Wow! It's lucky I had my scooter!

I've brought my journal right up to date, and now I *must* try to get a few hours sleep. Tomorrow will be a very busy day. Am I going to be stuck down here forever? I'll write more later.

Watch out →

Yikes!

Bron has got really long, curved claws.

I haven't had any sweets for four hundred years!

YUM YUM

Buzzzz! The killer bees are coming, so watch out.

How far away is home?

HOME ? MILES

Will I ever get out of this deep chasm?

Giant crabs are giant twits.   — Oh, yeah.

The Swarm!

The following morning Bron said we needed to get more honey.

"Verrry ... dangerrrous," he snarled, so I decided to check my rucksack to make sure I hadn't lost anything vital from my explorer's kit. This is what it contains:

1) My multi-tooled penknife
2) A ball of string
3) A telescope
4) This journal
5) A pack of wild animal collector's cards (full of amazing animal facts)
6) A glass eye from a steam-powered rhinoceros
7) The compass and torch I found on the dried-out skeleton of a lost explorer

8) The tooth of a monstrous megashark
9) A magnifying glass
10) A long length of vine I use as a lasso
11) My mobile phone with wind-up charger
12) A battered water bottle.

Magnifying glass

It was all there, so I followed Bron to the back of the cave where we climbed up a long, narrow crack in the rocks into an enormous cave above. One wall was pitted with the small cave mouths I'd seen from outside. The opposite wall was oozing streams of thick, golden honey.

"Wow! It's a honeycomb!" I whispered. "Imagine the size of the bees that made that!"

"Killerrr bees," warned Bron, quickly scooping up a pawful of honey and

The honeycomb ran with delicious honey.

stuffing it into his mouth. I looked nervously around as I dipped my finger in the sugary goo. Mmmm, it was delicious. I was just helping myself to seconds when a throbbing hum came from outside.

"Grrr, hide!" snarled Bron.

We ducked behind a boulder just as a swarm of bees flew in through the cave mouths. I gasped in astonishment. The bug-eyed monsters were as big as overstuffed pillows, with fat yellow bellies ringed with black warning stripes. They had horrible curved jaws that opened and closed threateningly. Their antennae waved about as they scanned the air for signs of trouble, and their deadly stingers were as long as swords.

The noise was incredible, like a thousand chainsaws buzzing. I clamped my hands over my ears as they hovered in front of the honeycomb, dropping sticky nectar from their wriggling legs. Then, as they turned to buzz out of the cave again, I had a sudden flash of inspiration.

I grabbed the vine lasso from my explorer's kit.

"Quick, Bron. Follow me," I whispered, as the bees flew towards the exits like a squadron of attack helicopters. I ran from behind the boulder, spinning the lasso around my head. I let it go and the vine snaked through the air, looping itself *I threw the vine lasso.* around the backside of one of the bees as it disappeared through an opening.

"Quick! On my back!" I yelled to Bron, as I was lifted from the ground. The bear ran and leaped, clamping himself onto my back with his long claws. *Yeeow!*

Flight Of The Bumblebees

We crashed into the side of the cave mouth, but were then pulled through it as the bee flew outside and up into the air. I looked down as we spun around and around above the bottomless chasm below.

"Yikes!" I cried, as a petrified Bron clamped his massive paws over my eyes and nearly crushed my head like a melon. "Get off, Bron," I cried. "I need to see where we're going."

The bee rose towards the top of the chasm, getting angrier and angrier as his wings whined from the strain of carrying two extra passengers. He jabbed his stinger at us, but couldn't reach and buzzed with frustrated fury. Then, *oh no!* He steered towards the side of the chasm where the crabs had chased me – and there they still were, leaning over the edge and snapping their crushing claws like castanets!

"No! Go the other way," I yelled, bouncing up and down on the end of the vine, but of course it made no difference. I was being taken back to where I'd started! I had no time to lose. Looking desperately around me, I saw a large shrub growing from the other side of the chasm (the side we wanted to be) and it was *just* in range.

I extended my right arm on which I wore my special Jakeman Spider-thread Wristband (here is Jakeman's diagram of it):

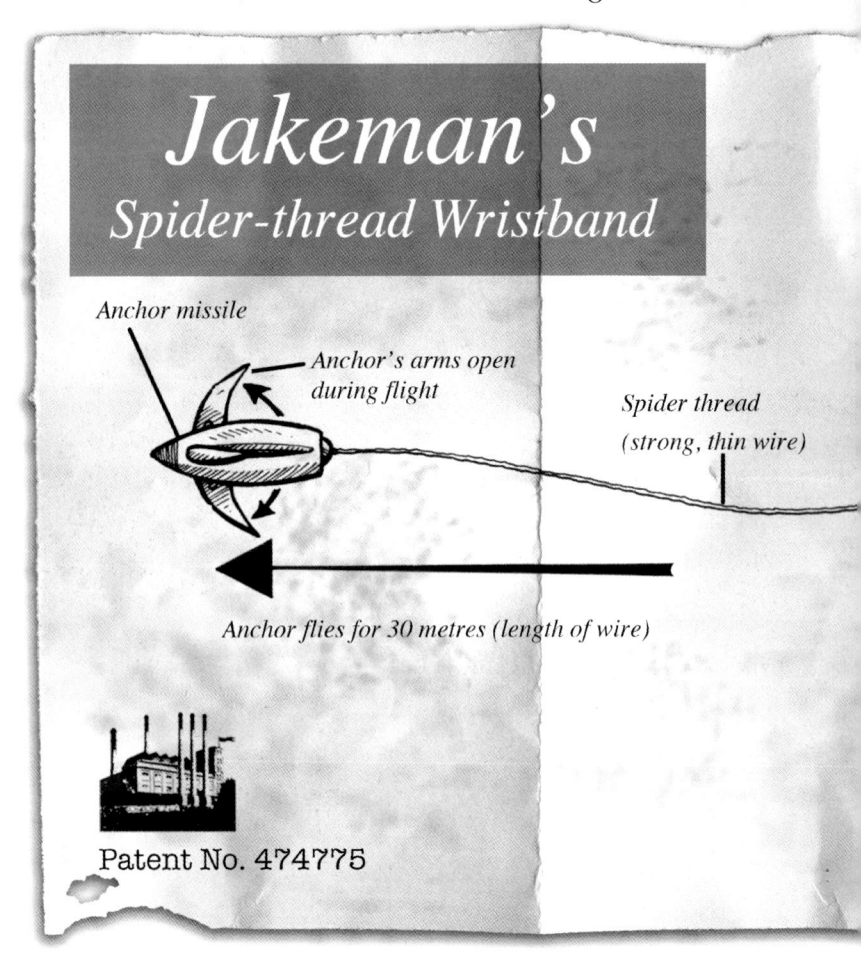

Jakeman's
Spider-thread Wristband

Anchor missile

Anchor's arms open during flight

Spider thread (strong, thin wire)

Anchor flies for 30 metres (length of wire)

Patent No. 474775

The wristband has a small metal anchor attached to a thin wire that winds around a powerful, motorised reel. Wrapping my

32

legs around the vine for support, I pressed the fire button with my left hand. The little anchor shot from my wrist like a

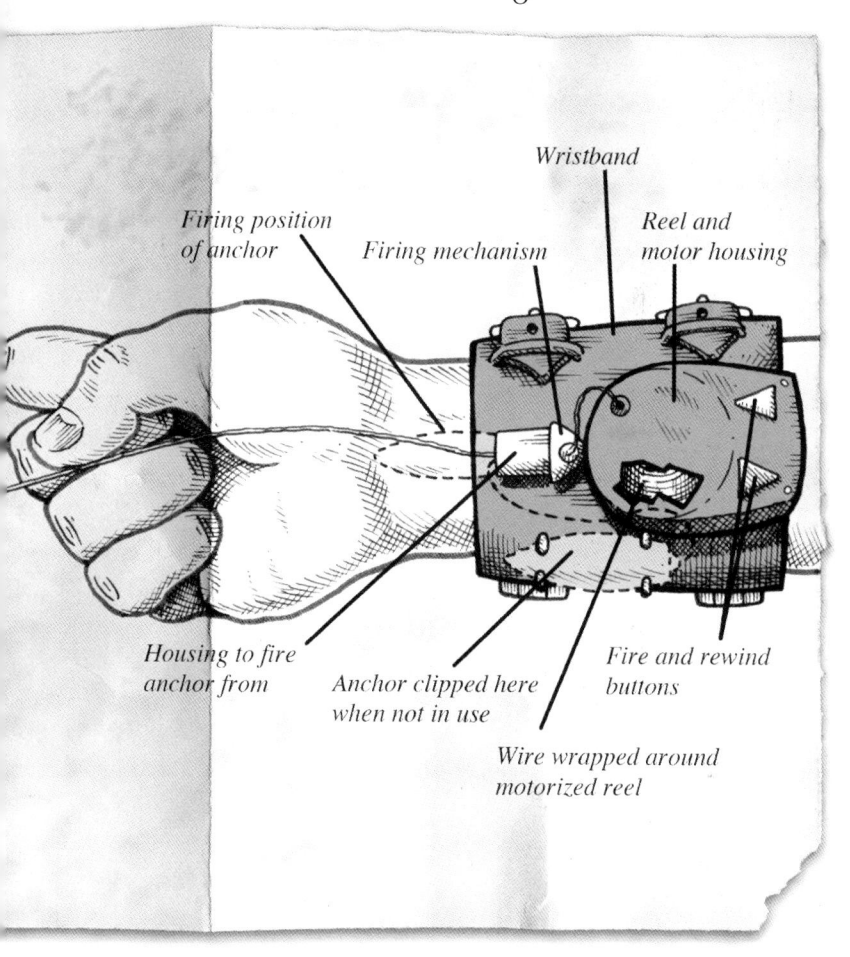

Firing position of anchor

Firing mechanism

Wristband

Reel and motor housing

Housing to fire anchor from

Anchor clipped here when not in use

Fire and rewind buttons

Wire wrapped around motorized reel

bullet. It clattered amongst the branches of the shrub and lodged tight.

"Hold on, Bron," I cried, and let go of

33

the vine. *"Geronimo!"*

We swung away from the bee on the end of our wire, straight towards the tall cliff face of the chasm. *Yikes!* Luckily, the shrub grew out of an overhanging part of the chasm, so we didn't smash into it. We swung wildly back and forth like a pendulum above the bottomless drop. I pressed another button. The motor in my wristband started to reel in the wire and Bron and I were hoisted up towards the shrub.

← Shrub

↑ Overhang

← Wire

↖ Bron and I were lifted up.

I grabbed the shrub's lower branches and climbed up onto the top of the chasm.

"Brilliant! We made it!" I whooped.

"Grrrreat!" growled Bron. Then, "Grrr!" he warned. I whirled around to see that the giant bee was zooming towards us, looking for revenge.

The Sting Is Mightier Than The Sword

Bzzzzz! Still trailing the length of vine the bee dived, bottom first, swishing its deadly stinger through the air. I drew my broken sword and so began a deadly swordfight!

Crash! Clatter! The bee whipped and whirled its stinger like an expert fencer, and I had to use all my pirate skills to avoid being injected with a deadly dose of bee-sting. It drove me backwards towards the edge of the chasm and I ducked and

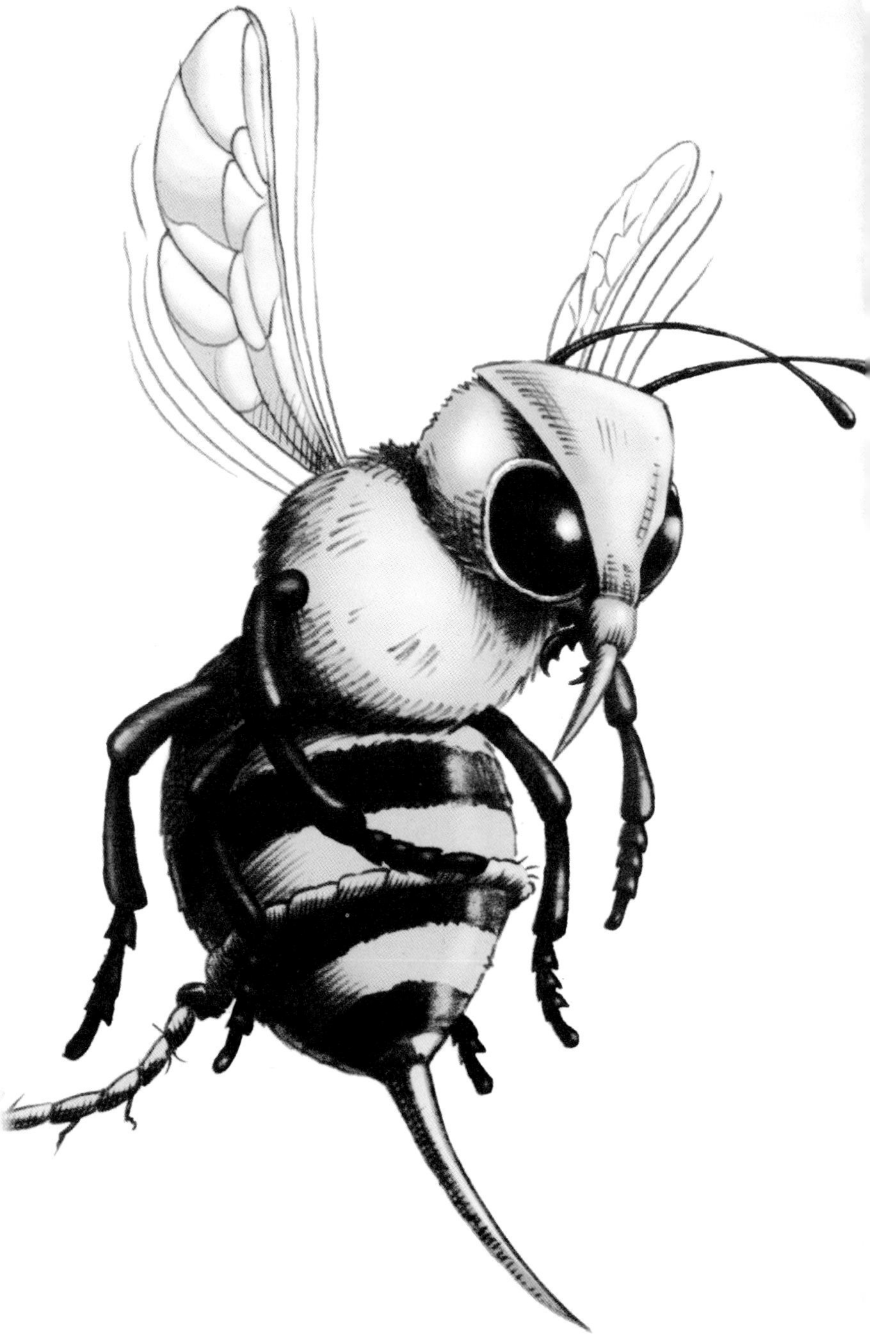

turned as its stinger whistled centimetres from my head.

"Come on, if you think you're good enough," I cried, and the bee dived once more. *Clash!* Again I fought, but my sword was very heavy and my arms were beginning to feel like lead.

Bron saw my problem and tried to help. He picked up a lump of rock and chucked it at the bee. With a twist of its wings, the insect dodged it and dived towards the bear, its stinger flashing in the sunlight.

Bron stood his ground but he had no weapon. The bee dived from the sky towards him. I leaped between them, raised my sword and smashed away the sting just as it reached Bron. The bee was knocked sideways, the sword clattered from my hand and I crashed to the ground, winded and gasping for breath.

The stinger hovered just above me.

The bee shook itself and came in for the kill. Knowing I was defeated, it paused for a moment in triumph before delivering its deadly sting. I shut my eyes and waited for the pain.

Pa!

ROAR! The air vibrated with a deafening bellow and the bee stopped in surprise, hovering just centimetres above me. I looked up, and there, not ten paces away, was the biggest, meanest bear I'd ever seen. Its great head swayed from side to side on a massive neck and its huge jaws drooled with saliva.

It swayed up onto its back legs and lumbered towards us. YIKES! It was at least three metres tall and its mighty paws were armed with claws like carving knives. With a terrific swipe, the bear walloped the bee. The insect went spinning across the chasm and landed in a buzzing daze on the other side.

"Pa!" yelled Bron, and leaped into his father's arms.

"Grrr, you grrr made it," said the adult bear, his deep voice rumbling like distant thunder.

"Yes. This is Charrrrlie. He rrrescued me," said Bron.

"Thank you, Charrrlie," growled his pa, and gave me a pat on the back with an enormous paw that sent me rolling across the ground.

"Oh, it was nothing," I gasped, trying to regain my breath.

"Sorrrry," said the bear with a throaty

chuckle as I got up and brushed the dust from my clothes. "We must go," he growled to Bron. "Ma's worrrried sick. Join us Charrrlie," he said. "We've got rrraw fish guts for brrreakfast."

Fish guts for brekkie? No thanks!

"Um, no, thank you," I said. I was hungry, but not *that* hungry. "I really must get on with my journey. I'm on my way home and Mum's expecting me for tea."

The happy bears lumbered away. As I had one last look at the awful chasm, I noticed something dangling from the crumbled remains of the bridge. It was my trusty Air-rider. How amazing is that! It was dented but still in working order.

I revved its engine and scooted away. In the distance, through a line of trees, I could see a huge, gushing river. *Oh boy,* I thought. *I wonder what adventures I will have next.*

I'll write more later, so look out for my other journals!

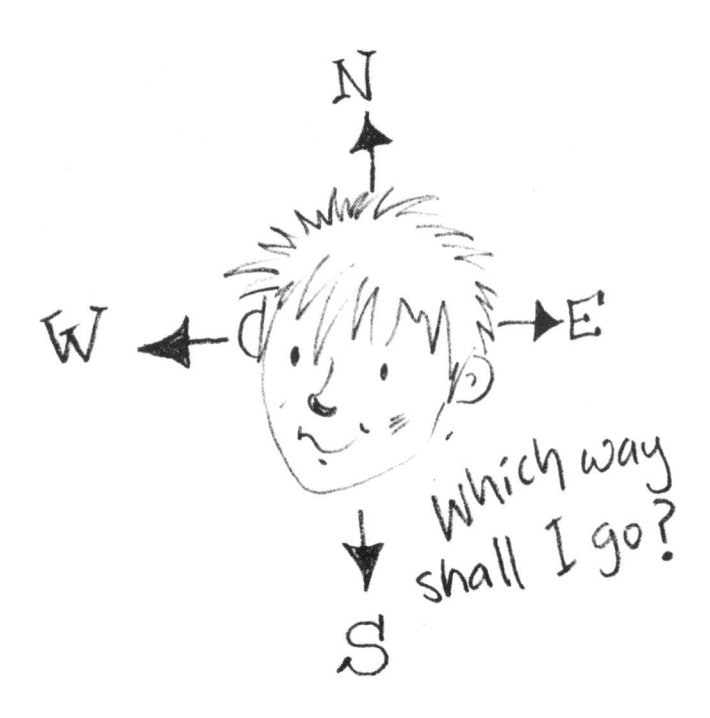

Which way shall I go?

Bron's pawprint

My Top Ten ~~Super~~ Heroes

1) Spiderman
2) ~~Batman~~ Dr Who
3) Sherlock Holmes
4) Tintin
5) Batman
6) Dan Dare (in my dad's old comics)
7) Robin Hood
8) Dr Syn The Scarecrow (from my Grandad's old books)
9) Zorro
10) Superman

I like Tarzan too!

My wish List

Things I wish I'd packed in my explorer's kit:

1) More food, especially chocolate
2) ~~Most~~ ~~Mosquee~~ Mozzy spray
3) Change of underwear
4) My game console
5) An explorer's hand book
6) ~~Compass~~ (got one off the skeletal explorer)
7) A butterfly net, for collecting new species
8) A pencil sharpener
9) ~~~~ A sleeping bag.

DANGER DANGER
HIGHLY TOXIC!

WARNING

Do not touch
This is some **KILLER**
BEE sting **POISON**
that got on my journal!

Watch out—there are monsters ahead!